To:

From:

mom
2
mom

**7 Reasons to be Grateful
You're the Mother of a** toddler

*Karen Sjoblom*

New Leaf Press
*A Division of New Leaf Publishing Group*

## 7 Reasons to be Grateful You're the Mother of a Toddler

First Printing: December 2006

ISBN-13: 978-0-89221-652-9
ISBN-10: 0-89221-652-2
Library of Congress Catalog Number: 2006937327

Cover and Interior Design: LeftCoast Design, Portland, OR 97219
Printed in Italy

For information regarding author interviews, please contact the publicity department at (870) 438-5288.

Please visit our website for other great titles:
www.newleafpress.net

## table of contents

To Betty Lou Blue Eyes—

High as the sky, deep

as the ocean . . . I love you.

**CHAPTER 1**

# Gratefulness

means we get a

do-over day

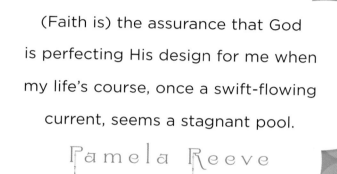

(Faith is) the assurance that God is perfecting His design for me when my life's course, once a swift-flowing current, seems a stagnant pool.

Pamela Reeve

*Faith Is*

F oot Book? Foot Book?" Emma asked hopefully as she
followed me around the house, toting a well-worn
copy of Dr. Seuss's classic. We'd read it so many times
I heard it in my nightmares. What I needed, though, was a
Butt Book: *wet butt, dry butt, low butt, high butt.*

Emma had caught a stomach bug and was ripping
through diapers as fast as I changed them, emitting such

robust and otherworldly noises in the process that I swore I saw little trails of steam wafting above her leggings. So it only made sense that the dog should have gotten into something in the yard and have diarrhea as well. I found myself chasing *him* with a diaper wipe, muttering, "If I have to clean anyone else's *butt* . . ."

On Diarrhea Day, I was feeling pretty sorry for myself . . .

That day, it was not good to be Queen.

In the early days of raising kids, I think we moms find ourselves seemingly living the same day over and over again. The carousel of laundry and diapers and meals and cleaning had completely eroded my sense that I was ever anything but a hausfrau. It collided against the memories of sitting in business meetings, being asked my *opinion*—getting *paid* for it, for Pete's sake—and I can't say that realization was without fallout.

On Diarrhea Day, I was feeling pretty sorry for myself, schlepping the laundry baskets up and down the stairs and taking the especially stinky diapers outside. I was resenting my husband for getting to talk to grown-ups at work, for not having to mop up bodily fluids all day long. And as I fumed in my head, I suddenly realized the house was calm except for some quiet babbling coming from the living room downstairs.

I sat on the landing and looked down. Emma had spread all of her books on the floor and was "reading" to herself, quietly. I left the laundry and got the video camera, and sat

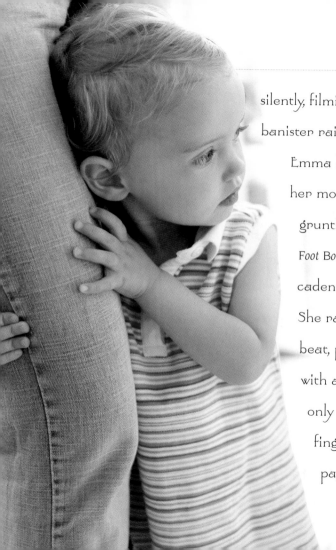

silently, filming between the
banister rails.

Emma had her pacifier in
her mouth and thus was
grunting the words to *The
Foot Book*. She knew the
cadence, the intonation.
She raised her feet to the
beat, pulling out the bink
with a satisfying *thwack!*
only to lick her little
fingers and turn the
page. The dog,

snoring away on top of the pile of lift-a-flap books and alphabet cards, thumped his tail once or twice as Em stopped reading to give him a little pat. I videotaped silently for about 15 minutes, just enjoying the quiet and the peace.

A wise woman once told me to look at these times in mothering for what they are: moments. There are good moments and hard moments, but still they are called *moments* and gratefully not *hairy, endless stretches of time.* Just moments.

Some do-over days come with repetition, with illness, with boredom, with questions, but thankfully ours is a God of second chances and more. It will most likely be good to be Queen again.

Perhaps tomorrow.

## **Gratefulness**

says a sense of humor is

the best medicine

There was a time when Emma was kind of afraid of men
and we worked on trying to help her feel a little more
comfortable in those situations. So when my friend and
I were at the local kiddie pool with our daughters and I glanced
over at Emma and saw her practically sitting in a man's lap,
my jaw dropped. And then I heard Emma say to this gentleman,
"Hi, my name is Emma and I have beautiful blue eyes."

I was mortified. I was already fast-forwarding in my mind, seeing her in a seedy bar someday, *Lolita* tattooed on her arm, using the same tired line. My girlfriend laughed and laughed, and I rolled my eyes at the man, who was also laughing. I walked over to them, suggested Emma go play in the water and said, "You don't mind setting an extra place for her tonight, do you?"

Kids can be so incredibly *literal*. I try to remember myself that way at one time, before life and logic crept in, but it seems a million miles away now. Thankfully I have Emma—

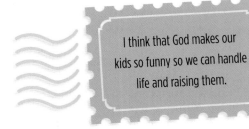

I think that God makes our kids so funny so we can handle life and raising them.

she of the beautiful blue eyes—to remind me to keep in the here and

now. She's the one who taught me solemnly that Jesus was the

greatest king in all the Pride Lands; this I call "Emma Logic" in

which Disney's *The Lion King* collides with King James.

I think that God makes our kids so funny so we can handle

life and raising them. There is much repetition in our daily routines—the kind that can make a capable woman start to talk to herself—that we need to have good belly-buckling, tear-streaming laughs. Often.

I told my girlfriend that this wasn't the first time that Emma dropped such a bomb. She said, "Didn't I tell you about the last time we were in Seattle?"

She and her husband had been teaching their daughter, Deanna, to cross the street safely by playing a game they called "white man/red hand"; the traffic signal icons show a red hand to stay put and a white man when it's safe to cross. They all were out with Deanna's aunt, who's married to a fairly dark-complexioned man from India. As he started to cross the inter-section against the light, Deanna started pointing and screaming at his general vicinity, "Not a white man! Not a white man!"

I roared. There's nothing like a toddler to point out the obvious.

Sandwiches! Sandwiches! Bears are eating Hunan Sandwiches!

Later that day, we relaxed over some lunch and a little *Pocahontas*. Late in the movie, the two warring sides accuse each other of being "savages" and "barely even human"—of not understanding what is sacred to each group. I heard Emma singing along and did a double-take:

*Sandwiches! Sandwiches! Bears are eating Hunan Sandwiches!*

Three belly laughs today. I have been blessed.

## CHAPTER 3

## Gratefulness

means we are thankful that

God has a plan

A friend left a message on my answering machine that said, "Don't forget, God loves us exactly the way we are, and God loves us too much to let us stay like this." Only I think she must have misquoted it, because she said, "God loves you too much to let you stay like this."

Anne Lamott

*Traveling Mercies*

If God intended our children's performance to define our worth, He would have given us fully grown, college-educated, upstanding citizens with tastefully matted Nobel medals above their antique cherry desks.

I learned this the hard way when Emma was almost two. I'd had dinner with someone whose daughter is the same age, and I'd always felt this weird competition, as if we had to prove whose child was superior. When she coached her

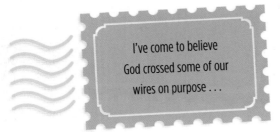

I've come to believe
God crossed some of our
wires on purpose . . .

daughter to recite her numbers through ten, I smiled and said she did a very good job. But *wait*, my friend says. *There's more!!* So I listened again...in Spanish. And French. And Japanese.

So I glanced at Emma, who, nonplussed, was maneuvering a banana into her ear.

She'd missed the whole thing.

After we'd gotten home, I wondered whether I could teach

Emma, "O Mother, light of my being" in some ancient dialect—
and how quickly—when I suddenly welled up.

This child, with her angel curls and sunny disposition, could
give a rat's fanny about her numbers right now. I felt ashamed
for thinking she was lacking. *She* knows she's enough . . . A *fresh
diaper, a cup of juice and thou.* Why wasn't it OK with me?

And then I got it: the wondering whether I'm enough for *her*. The question of whether God pulled the wrong file when He assigned me, with all my angst, to mother this child. So I peered into the mirror God holds up, kindly, smiling—the one that reflects all my shortcomings—and realized what He's teaching me, via Emma, is the wisdom of stillness—and time. And stranger yet, He's OK with where I'm at today.

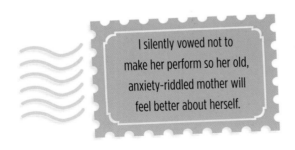

I silently vowed not to make her perform so her old, anxiety-riddled mother will feel better about herself.

In this life, we're going to feel we're not *something* enough—that we're lacking, we're stumbling, we're failing. But I've come to believe God crossed some of our wires on purpose, so we might learn Who we're living for, in addition to the hows and whys. In our weakness, Strength.

Later that evening, Emma gently placed her hand on my cheek and gave a pat, kindly. And I looked at her through the eyes of a woman who knows in her soul that it'll be OK because of the One with the Plan. I silently vowed not to make her perform so her old, anxiety-riddled mother will feel better about herself. And if I can keep this promise to her even half the time, she will be light years ahead of me.

Where she belongs.

## CHAPTER 4

**Gratefulness**

means we are thankful

for the people in our lives

Just then, Ollie started to cry. Grampa Miller looked weary of that boy . . . "Don't worry, Grampa. I know how to calm this baby down," I said. After that, I patted Ollie's back very nice. Then I hummed real soft in his ear. And I put him in the hall closet.

Junie B.

*First Grader, Toothless Wonder, Barbara Park*

She'd been married forever, infertile for six years and a mom for four weeks. Her voice broke a bit on the phone as she struggled to give words to her feelings: She was exhausted, weepy, overwhelmed; everyone told her she should be ecstatic because she and her husband had to wait so long.

So I told her of the night when Emma was six weeks old.
I fed her, I burped her, I sang to her and, as I laid her gently
in her crib, I told her, softly, lovingly, that if she didn't sleep
through the night she was going to live in the garage.

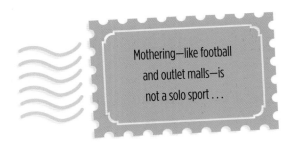

Mothering—like football
and outlet malls—is
not a solo sport . . .

"Really?"
my friend said,
sniffling, barely
hopeful. "Tell me
more . . ."

Why is it that moms feel we can't tell the truth about how
impossible our jobs can be at times? Yes, we love them to death
and we'd tear to shreds anything that threatened them—
including ourselves. Some of my worst moments as a human

being have happened while
mothering...times when I thought
it would be difficult to behave
more poorly, react more insanely, judge more
harshly. What I really need to do is spill my guts to the people
in my life—the ones who have enough experience, distance,
and frankly, bias to help me out of the pit.

Mothering—like football and outlet malls—is not a solo
sport. Much as we'd like to save face or flog ourselves inwardly
for our perceived lack of motherly love, if we're going to make
it long-term, we've got to utter those awful thoughts to another.

We're lost, we're tired, we're crazily unfulfilled living the exact same day over and over. We're tired of our kitchen floors looking like gridded petri dishes. We've lost our purpose, our compass. We used to *be* somebody—don't you get it?—somebody with briefcases, offices, ideas, *benefits* . . . .

I've found it just takes a little crack—a little chink in your veneer where you're willing to let a little of your darkness out —and the stories flow forth from all directions. Tempers shot, memories marred, tongues sharp—the stories come and we get the humanness of all of it. Taking that step paved the way for more conversations—ones that included hard questions, soft resolve, quiet tears, loud fears. I think God plopped these women in my life so I wouldn't marathon alone on that rat wheel in my brain.

With His mercy, you'll find a group of fabulous women, as stunned and incompetent as you, each with a plethora of awful thoughts. If you're lucky, many of these thoughts will be far more awful than the ones *you* think, and the weight will fall away as your laughter fills the space.

CHAPTER
5

## Gratefulness

means we thank God

for the job

...on the

deepest level,

service is an experience of belonging,

an experience of connection to others and to the

world around us. It is this connection that gives us the

power to bless the life in others. Without it, the life

in them would not respond to us.

Rachel Naomi Remen, MD

*My Grandfather's Blessings*

I hate to admit this, but I was the teensiest bit overprotective of Emma when she was little. I followed all the directions in the books (I would have sterilized the dog if he'd have let me) and I did all the "right" things but I kept her to myself. I'm reminded of a scene in the movie *Finding Nemo* when the seagulls were fighting over food, screeching "Mine! Mine! Mine!"

That's kind of how I felt about Emma.

In a feeble attempt to appear competent, I brushed aside the offers of help, the hands reaching toward us, the unsolicited but usually sound advice. Secretly, I think I was worried about job security: that I'd lose top ranking, that I wouldn't be needed. It never dawned on me that maybe I was *supposed* to loosen my grip a little...perhaps there was a need to share both of us with the outside world, and maybe even gain something in return.

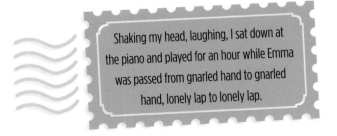

Shaking my head, laughing, I sat down at the piano and played for an hour while Emma was passed from gnarled hand to gnarled hand, lonely lap to lonely lap.

I called a local retirement center and asked

whether they'd like me to come and play piano once each week ... and could I bring my little daughter with me? The activity coordinator was thrilled and asked how soon I could come. The following Tuesday Emma and I arrived, unprepared for the

reception we received. Dozens of seniors were waiting for us in the lounge, and soon the banter began.

*Bring that child to me. It's my turn to hold her!*

*You like Grandma Betty best, don't you, sweet girl?*

*Betty! You're hogging my child!*

Shaking my head, laughing, I sat down at the piano and played for an hour while Emma was passed from gnarled hand to gnarled hand, lonely lap to lonely lap. Apparently, the

music was fine but the toddler was the real draw. I was asked repeatedly, "You're coming back next week, right?"

And we did. And each week, Emma's fan club was there to greet her. Our favorite

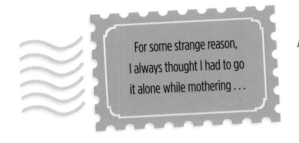

For some strange reason, I always thought I had to go it alone while mothering . . .

was Arlene, a tiny Jewish grandma who'd sneak Emma food each visit: "Honey?" she'd whisper conspiratorially to Emma, "Lemme put some buttah on that for ya . . ."

My stint there lasted almost two years, and Emma and I found ourselves blessed; between the music and the conversations and the 67 extra grandparents, I reclaimed a side of myself that had been lost, and found my mommy job that much more doable.

For some strange reason, I always thought I had to go it alone while mothering, like I was somehow failing my job description by leaning on others. I now realize how foolish that was, barricading myself under the guise of "doing a good job." What I found was a whole new generation, wise in ways that made me take pause, that really made me thank God for the job . . . and that I didn't have to do it alone.

## CHAPTER 6

**Gratefulness**

means we thank God

for our strengths

and weaknesses

God gave all humans—His supreme creation—
considerable freedom, and that includes
the opportunity to goof up.

Foster Cline, MD,
and Jim Fay

*Parenting with Love and Logic*

I am genetically prompt. It's in my DNA; I am early for practically everything. So as Emma and I drove at 4:45 am to the airport for our first solo trip, I was horrified to discover I had terribly miscalculated the time we needed to get on the plane.

Pre-911, you could screech up to the gate with 20 seconds to spare. That's about all we had after a long sprint with Emma bouncing in my arms, asking, "Ma. Ma. Are. We. O.K.?"

Lowering myself into my seat, breathless, I tried to relax. I am a Plan Girl—the more detailed, the better. Rarely do I react with "What a charming and whimsical deviation!" I was feeling kind of scared traveling alone anyway and kicked into Hypervigilant Mode, which upped the tension.

I've asked God about a million times why He made me the way He did: why I can get so rattled over stupid things, why I can't just chill out. I think He laughs at me—I really do. Because with the drama, He also pumped me full of humor and mercy, creativity and encouragement. When we become moms, we also become keenly aware of our shortcomings. Post-child(ren), we don't appear nearly as put together as we did before. So I'm learning to stop and pause at my weaknesses, turn them over and remember to look at what lies beyond.

By our layover at Dallas/Fort Worth, I hadn't lost Emma, or the carry-ons, or my mind, so the day was looking up. But in the bathroom, Emma told me she wanted *privacy* because she's a *big girl* now. So I let her go into the stall by herself while I waited outside. Vigilantly. And as toddlers do, she took her sweet time acting all

I've asked God about a million times why He made me the way He did . . .

potty trained, and I waited. And waited. And I was starting to get pissy again because, darn it, we had another plane to catch and lunch to eat and a gate to find.

While I was spinning in my head, I heard Emma jump off the toilet to get redressed. That's when we learned that DFW toilets flush *automagically*. She *flew* out of that stall, Pull-Ups® and leggings around her ankles, because, after all, it was the end of her world as she knew it—that great sucking *whoosh* she wasn't anticipating. It was classic. And I started to laugh. And laugh. And she saw me laugh, so she started to giggle and looked at me as if to say, "I sure wasn't expecting *that!*"

It was one of those moments when I realized I *can do this*. And I hold those images close, because for as many instances I've felt like a failure as a mom, there are also those snippets in time where you realize God really did give you the goods to do the job—highlights and lowlights, shadow and light.

## CHAPTER 7

# Gratefulness

means we thank God

for the journey

S oon after Emma was born, my mom came to help,
and one afternoon I'd put some music on the stereo
and slow-danced with this little bundle the size of a
bag of flour. James Taylor and I crooned "Rockabye, sweet
baby Em" while I performed a lumbering, post-C-section
waltz around the living room, my tears falling on her face.

I looked over to my mom, who was pretending to read the paper but crying, obviously moved by the pork recipe in the food section. Here we were, three generations, just stumbling around, trying to find our way. Maybe that's one of the big reasons people decide to have kids—the idea of getting it *right* this time. Certainly, during my first dance with Em, I didn't know what I know now—that there's no getting it "right" ever—but it was one of those sweet moments when all eternity is open to the possibility.

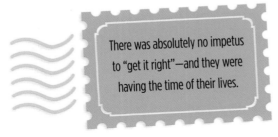

There was absolutely no impetus to "get it right"—and they were having the time of their lives.

Fast forward a couple of years, and I'm at Emma's first ballet recital.

What struck me most about the evening weren't the little dancers with their baby bellies protruding over their tutus, but the amazing lessons I gained from my daughter. During the performance, there were girls peering into the audience, waving, daydreaming, poking each other, and generally not paying attention. There was absolutely no impetus to "get it right"—and they were having the time of their lives.

Like many daughters, I have at times wrestled with my relationship

with my mom—wanting to "get it right" and failing miserably. I was raised to perform well, and it's taken me years to be able to let up a bit, to settle for less than perfection. Gratefully, I've learned on this particular journey—that of raising children—it is far better to do a little worse, if you know what I mean. On recital night, I watched Emma blow kisses to the audience and realized all was right in her world—she had no illusions that any of it had to be perfect.

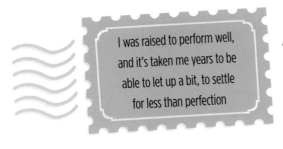

I was raised to perform well, and it's taken me years to be able to let up a bit, to settle for less than perfection

In our pas de deux, I lead...for now. But there will come a time when Em will jockey for position, when we won't understand each other, when doors will slam and words will sting. But as I've learned with my own mom, that journey can come full circle if you'll let it, ending near

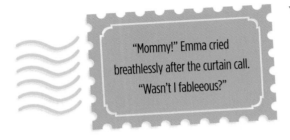

"Mommy!" Emma cried breathlessly after the curtain call. "Wasn't I fableeous?"

where you began but with a whole lot more understanding and grace than you had when you took the first step. And it doesn't have to be flawless.

"Mommy!" Emma cried breathlessly after the curtain call. "Wasn't I *fableeous*?" Her eyes, wide and hopeful, took in the pride on my face. "Baby, you were brilliant," I said. She clapped her hands gleefully, and I took all of her in: the joy, the innocence, the ribbons and tulle. I will cherish this image on the journey like a time-worn photograph—the pureness of it, the perfect imperfection of it.

We're thankful you've chosen to explore

*7 Reasons to be Grateful You're the Mother of a Toddler.*

If these essays have made you recall your own

for-better-or-worse moments, take a few minutes

to write some thoughts to perhaps share with your

child(ren) sometime ... like after they have their *own* kids.

## How Many Do-Over Days Can We Have?

Sometimes during a long string of seemingly wasted days, we long for meaning, purpose, and some guarantee this child-rearing gig will turn out positively. Is there a time you can look back on, now from a different perspective, when the dreariness of day-to-day family duties produced a bit of hope after a long, dry spell?

## ⋯⋯⋯ When Your Sense of Humor is Buried Beneath Your Laundry...

Immediately following 9/11, New York Mayor Rudy Giuliani suggested we needed to find a way to laugh again—while we're still crying. Some might suggest this applies to motherhood as well. Can you recall some times when laughter gave way to tears . . . and tears gave way to laughter?

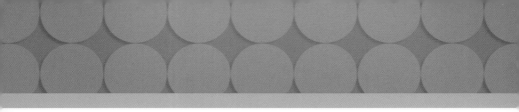

## What's the Master Plan?

It's been said that life has to be lived forward, but can only be understood backwards. As a mom, what experiences have you had that have shifted your view of your plans versus God's plans? In what areas are you still hoping your plans will win?

## ⬤⬤⬤⬤⬤⬤ Never Alone

As Hillary Clinton noted, it takes a village to raise a child. Who are the members of your tribe, your people? How have they helped you raise your family? In what areas do you feel you *have* to go it alone?

## It's a Tough Job, But Someone's Got to Do It...

Some say parenting is the only job for which we apply without a clue of what we're doing. Do you view parenting as a chore? A job? A gift? How has it been different from what you expected or hoped for?

Do you feel hand-picked by God to parent your specific kids? Does this notion change your view of your own strengths and weaknesses?

☆☆☆☆☆☆☆☆☆☆☆☆☆☆☆☆☆☆☆☆☆☆☆☆☆

# 888
## Reasons to Hate
# DEMOCRATS

☆☆☆☆☆☆☆☆☆☆☆☆☆☆☆☆☆☆☆☆☆☆☆☆☆